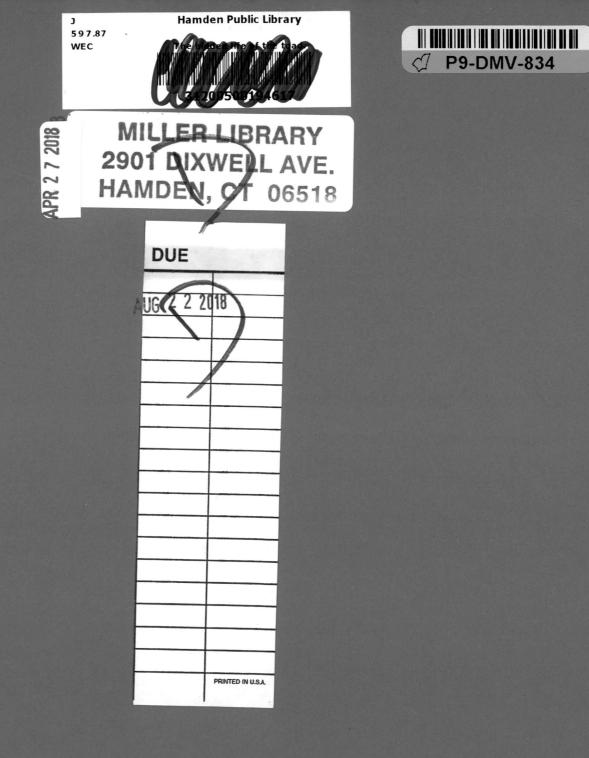

DUE

AUG 2 2 2018

PRINTED IN U.S.A.

The Hidden Life of a Toad

Doug Wechsler

i⚓i Charlesbridge

April sunshine warms a shallow pond.

In the water, strings of jelly

twist over, under, around.

What is this tangle of stuff?

It looks like a pile of spaghetti.

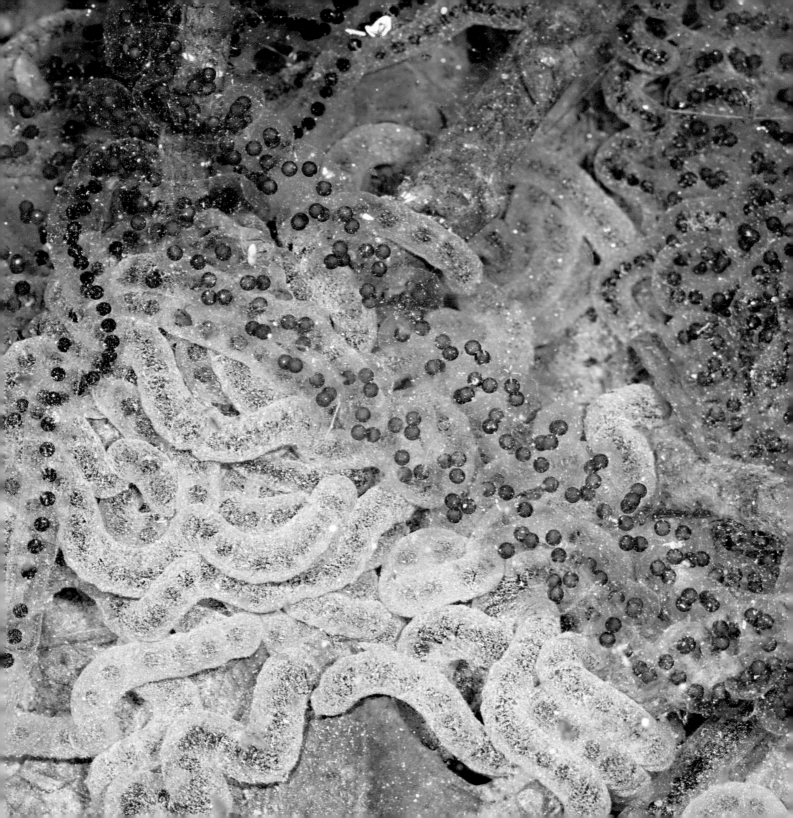

Day 1

Inside the strings,

tiny round eggs are trapped,

egg after egg after egg.

Each egg is a little black ball—

the embryo—

with more jelly around it.

One embryo would just fit inside this o.

Not ten,

not one hundred,

but thousands of embryos are lined up

in each string.

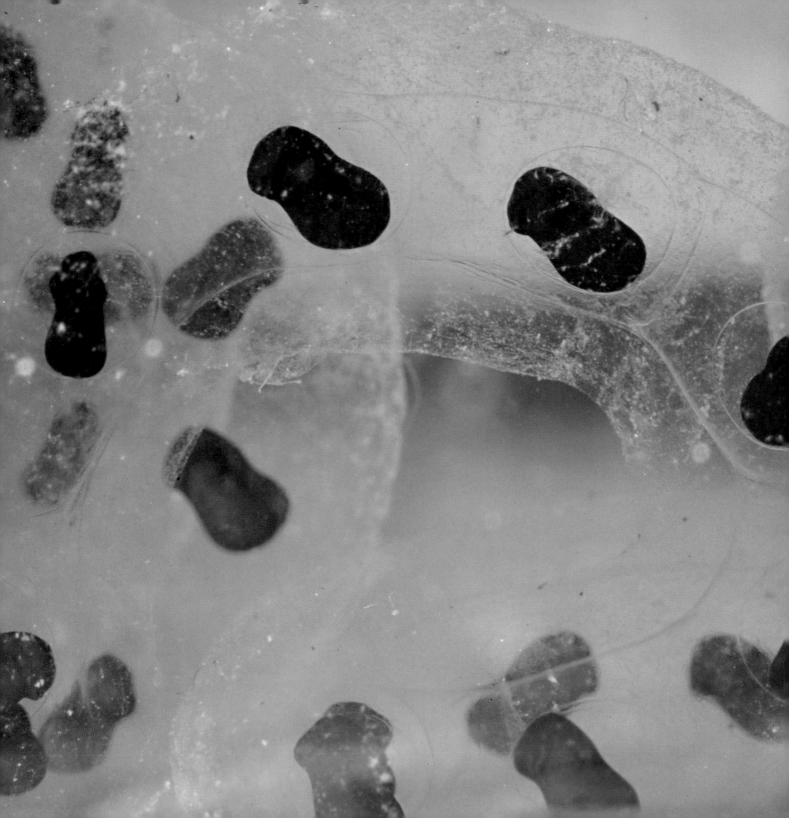

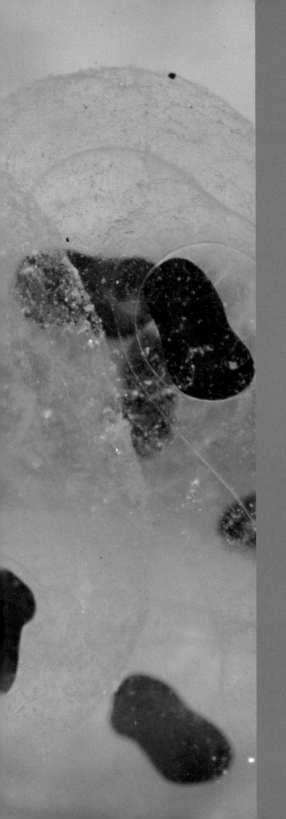

Day 3

Two days pass.

The embryos grow and take shape.

Each little black ball stretches.

Day 5

One embryo wiggles.

It wriggles.

It jiggles about.

A tiny tadpole slides out, free of the jelly.

It has no mouth.

It has no eyes.

It cannot even swim.

It waits on top of the coiled jelly string.

Its brothers and sisters by the thousands
struggle loose from their eggs.

Day 9

What a difference four days make!

Now the tadpole has eyes for seeing.

It has a big tail for swimming.

It has a mouth for munching

morsels of rotting leaves.

And for breathing?

Feathery gills,

those little frills behind the head,

pull oxygen from the water.

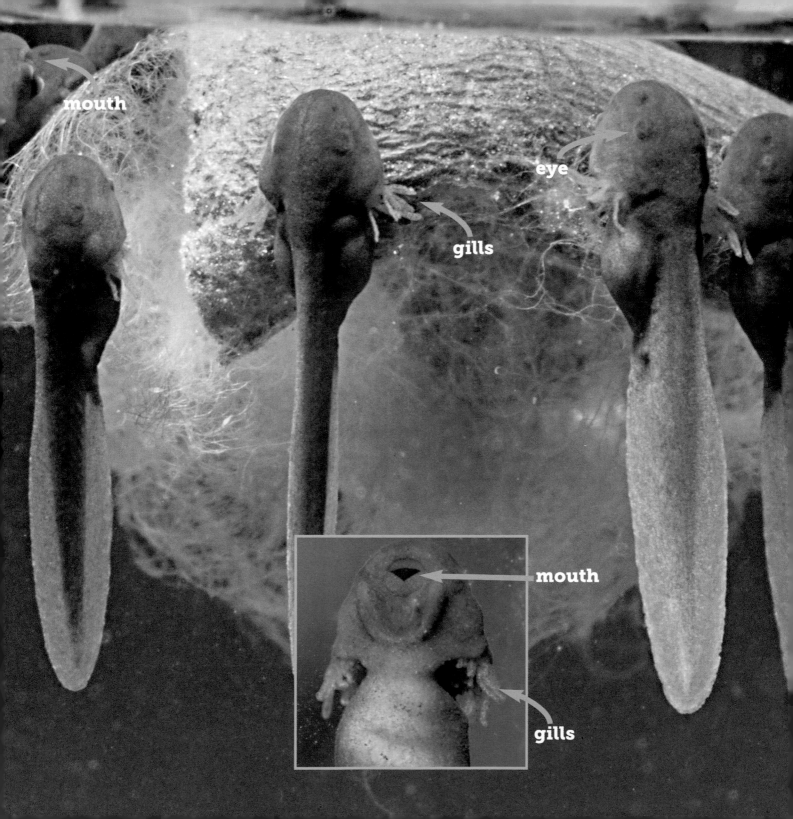

Day 12

Skin has grown over the graceful gills.
Water flows into the mouth,
over the gills,
and spews out a hole in the skin
called the spiracle.
Now the tadpole is fat and round in front,
with a long skinny tail behind.
It has the familiar tadpole shape.

spiracle

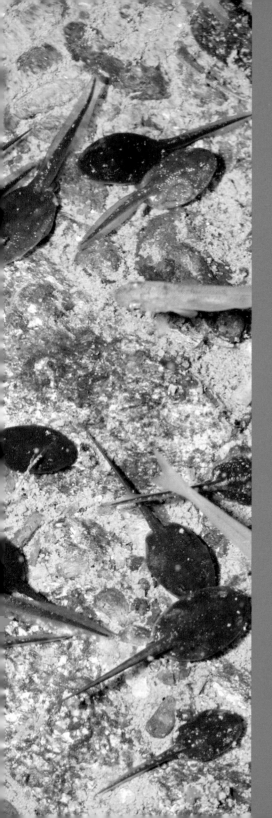

Day 20

Tiny tadpoles school
at the edge of the pond.
The water is warm here,
and too shallow for big, hungry fish.
Tadpoles grow fast in warm water.

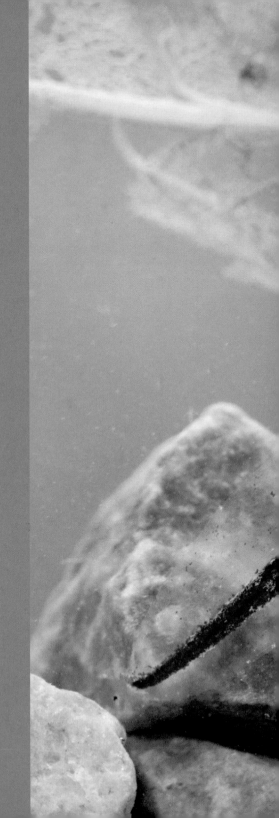

Day 27

Legs grow out.

Toes are forming.

Why would a tadpole need legs and toes?

Day 41

Arms bulge behind the mouth.

Pop! The right arm
breaks through the skin.

arm under skin

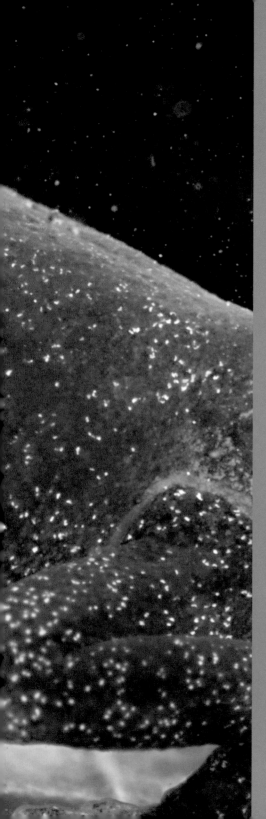

Psshh! The left arm pushes out
through the spiracle.
With four limbs,
the miracle of metamorphosis
is under way.
It's the big change
from tadpole to toadlet.

Day 45

The tadpole changes inside and out.

Its stomach swells.

The long, coiled intestine shortens.

Lungs grow.

Legs get strong and . . .

Day 47

. . . eyes bulge.

The mouth widens.

The tadpole is now a toadlet.

It moves to the shore.

The toadlet's tongue lengthens.

Its tail shrinks . . .

Day 49

. . . and disappears.

But the tail is not wasted.

It is recycled.

It breaks down inside the body,

releasing energy.

The toadlet grows longer and stronger

for the journey ahead.

Day 55

Time to look for a home.

The toadlet goes hopping,

hopping,

hopping

through the forest.

It is hardly bigger than a pea.

Day 70

A good home for a toad has

plenty of bugs and worms,

rocks to hide under,

leaves for shade, and

loose soil that's easy to dig.

The toadlet eats and grows

in the green garden.

On hot summer days

it buries itself to stay cool.

In fall it digs deep down into the dirt.

All through the long, cold winter,

it stays buried.

Each year it grows and grows.

Day 1097 (Year 3)

By the third spring
the toadlet has grown up.
She's a big, warty toad—
a fat female full of eggs.
Warm rains seep deep,
creeping into the soil
where the toad waits
in her winter hideout.
Suddenly she has an urge to travel.
Time to hop, hop, hop
to the pond where she was born.

Brrrrrrrrrrrrrrrrrrrrrrr!

A male toad trills from day into night.

His vocal sac swells like a balloon.

He sits in the shallow part of the pond,

sending a signal:

Come see me.

The distant female listens

to his ringing song.

vocal sac

Day 1098

Night falls.

The female hops, hops,

then plops into the pond.

The male swims onto her back.

Whack! He kicks another male

who tries to grab her.

Hold on tight!

She carries him through the night,

until . . .

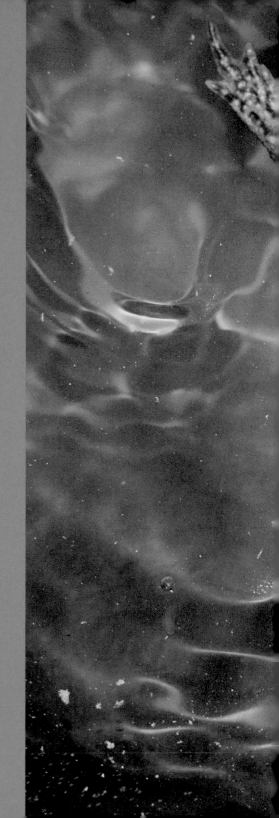

male

rival male

female

strings of eggs

male

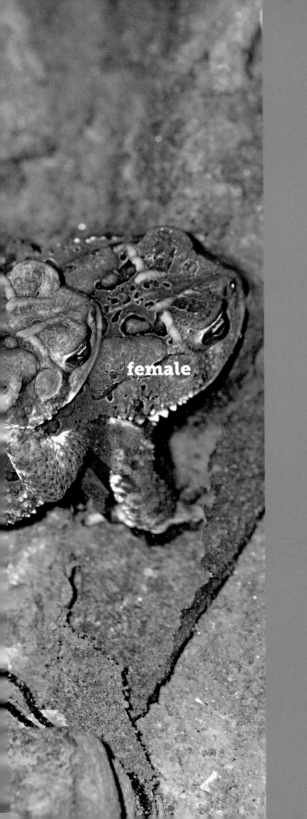

female

. . . she lays eggs in two long jelly strings.

The male fertilizes the eggs

as they come out.

The strings swell

as the jelly fills with water.

Now the female is no longer so plump.

She climbs out of the pond

and hops away.

But the male stays.

He sings again—*Brrrrrrrrrr!*

—and waits for another female.

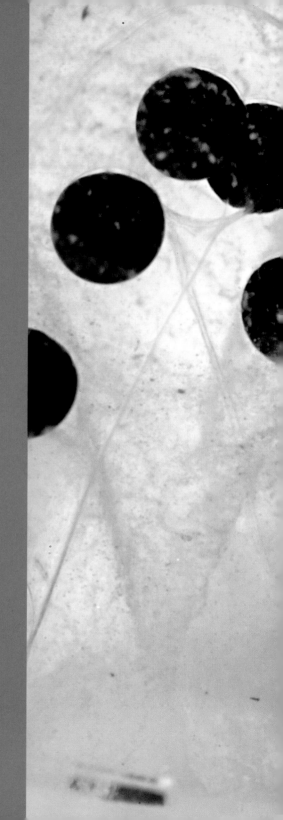

Day 1099

The female heads home,

hopping,

hopping,

hopping.

A new Day 1

Back in the pond, those little black balls—

the embryos—grow.

Then one day they wiggle.

They wriggle.

They jiggle about.

Thousands of tadpoles slide out,

free of the jelly.

A new cycle of life begins.

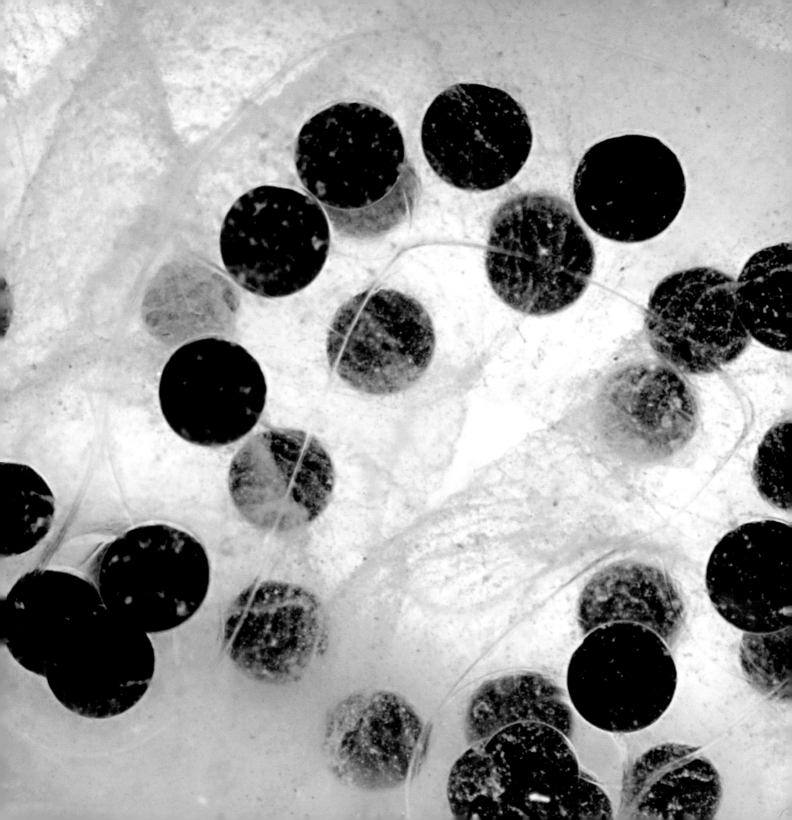

Glossary

embryo (EM-bree-oh): An animal developing inside its mother or inside an egg.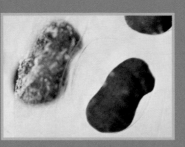

fertilize (FUR-tuh-lize): To make an egg start growing by adding a male cell. A fertilized egg will form an embryo.

 **gills** (GILZ) Feathery body parts that bring oxygen from the water into the bloodstream of an aquatic animal.

intestine (in-TES-tin): The long, thin part of the digestive system where food goes after leaving the stomach.

metamorphosis (meh-tah-MORE-fuh-sis): The big change from one life stage to another, very different stage, such as from tadpole to toadlet.

oxygen (AHK-si-jun): The gas in the air and water that animals need to breathe.

spiracle (SPIR-ih-kul): A breathing hole.

tadpole (TAD-pole): The early stage of life of a frog or toad.

 **toadlet** (TODE-let): A tiny toad that has just changed from a tadpole.

 **vocal sac** (VOH-kahl SAK): The part of a male toad's throat that expands like a balloon and helps broadcast its song.

What's the difference between a frog and a toad?

The easy answer: a frog has smooth, moist skin and jumps with its long legs; a toad has dry, warty skin and hops with its short legs.

But it's not so simple. All frogs and toads are amphibians—animals with backbones that (mostly) start life in water, breathing with gills, and later grow lungs and are able to move onto land. There are three main groups of amphibians: salamanders, worm-shaped creatures called caecilians (sah-SIL-yens), and anurans (ah-NOO-rahns). Frogs and toads belong to the last group, called Anura (ah-NOO-rah).

Scientists divide Anura into about two dozen groups, called families. One of those families is Bufonidae (boo-FAHN-eh-dee), the "true toads." This family includes the American toad, the subject of this book. Members of this family are usually (but not always) called toads.

Some anurans from other families are also called toads. Spadefoot toads and narrow-mouthed toads belong to other families and are not considered to be true toads. They are not closely related to true toads and have differences in their bones and some internal organs.

As far as scientists are concerned, frogs and toads are all anurans. That way, they don't have to decide which is which!

frog

toad

Toad Facts

- Adult American toads measure between 2.5 inches (6.4 centimeters) and 4 inches (10 centimeters) long. Female toads are larger than males.

- The scientific name for the American toad is *Anaxyrus americanus* (an-AX-ir-us ah-MER-eh-CAN-us), though you will see the name *Bufo americanus* (BOO-foh ah-MER-eh-CAN-us) in older books.

- A female American toad can lay up to 20,000 eggs in strings up to 60 feet (18 meters) long.

- The big bumps over a toad's eyes are parotoid (pur-AH-toyd) glands. They produce a milky liquid full of poisons. If a dog or fox bites a toad, it will spit the toad out. Swallowing the toad might be deadly.

parotoid gland

- Toad tadpoles also have poisons in their skin. This keeps some fish from eating them. That's why toads can breed in ponds and streams with fish, where many frogs won't breed.

- Toads do have some enemies. Garter snakes and hognose snakes can eat toads whole. Raccoons and crows leave the skin behind.

- Toads eat just about any moving animal that fits in their mouth: beetles, ants, moths, wasps, slugs, centipedes, and worms. A toad can eat hundreds of small insects in a day.

- A toad has no teeth; it swallows its prey whole.

- A toad sheds its skin, but it doesn't leave it behind like a snake. It swallows the skin as it sheds.

- A toad "drinks" water through its belly. It sits in a wet place and lets water soak through its skin.

- Toads will not give you warts, but their toxins can irritate mucous membranes (like the skin inside your nose), so wash your hands after holding a toad.

Saving Toads

Toads play an important role in our environment. They eat many harmful insects and are eaten by many other animals. It's also fun to watch and listen to them. Unfortunately, toad numbers have dropped in many places, as more roads and houses are built and more chemicals are used to kill insects and weeds. Toads need our help.

If you live near Philadelphia, you can help with Toad Detour. On the first few warm, wet nights of spring, thousands of toads cross a road in Philadelphia to get to a reservoir where they breed. Hundreds of toads were getting run over until a woman named Lisa Levinson noticed the problem and took action. In 2008 Lisa organized Toad Detour. At first, volunteers carried toads across the road. Then Lisa got the city's permission to close the road during toad migration nights. Now every year Toad Detour—and other conservation groups around the country—work to keep tens of thousands of toads and other amphibians safe.

Here are some more ways you and your family can help toads and other amphibians:

- Don't use poisons to kill insects or weeds in your yard or garden. Most of these poisons harm amphibians.

- Don't release pet amphibians or other pets into the wild. They can spread diseases to native amphibians.

- Keep cats indoors. They kill amphibians and many other small animals.

- Create a backyard pond without fish, where amphibians can safely breed.

- Use less energy by turning off lights, taking brief showers, and walking or biking instead of driving. Amphibian habitats are often polluted and destroyed when oil, coal, and natural gas are produced to make energy.

Getting the Photos

I have observed toads most of my life. But I really got to know them well when I decided to tell the story of their life cycle. I studied toads by both observing and reading. I learned what weather brings toads out in the spring. I had to move quickly, because most breeding takes place in just a few days.

Getting wet was part of the job. Toads move in wet weather. They also pee on you when you pick them up.

Back at home I cut my own glass to make a small aquarium. I then collected toad eggs and used special close-up lenses to photograph the developing embryos and tiny tadpoles.

This brought a big surprise. I thought a toad's arm grew out slowly from its body. Not so. After photographing the tadpole with the arm bulging beneath its skin, I waited hours to shoot the arm coming out. But the tricky tadpole swam out of sight for thirty seconds—and swam back with the arm already out!

Going out night after night, while everyone else is comfortable at home, can be tiring. But there have been many rewards. While searching for toads, I have heard the hoarse scream of a fox, the eerie screeches of raccoons, and the hollow hooting of horned owls.

Best of all, the toads are too busy calling, grabbing each other, and laying eggs to notice my flashlight beam. It's a wonderful way to enter their hidden world.

Books

Sweeney, Alyse. *Toads*. North Mankato, MN: Capstone, 2010.

Stewart, Melissa. *Frog or Toad? How Do You Know?* Berkeley Heights, NJ: Enslow, 2011.

Markle, Sandra. *Toad Weather*. Atlanta, GA: Peachtree, 2015.

Websites

www.dougwechsler.com/toad/toads.php
Visit my website for more photos and information about toads at home and around the world.

www.schuylkillcenter.org/programs/ public_events.html
Learn more about Toad Detour.

www.nhptv.org/natureworks/american toad.htm
Find out more about the life cycle of the American toad.

Range of the American Toad

To Lisa Levinson, Toad Detour founder,
and to Claire Morgan, who has carried the
Toad Detour torch for the Schuylkill Center
for Environmental Education

Acknowledgments

Many thanks to those whose invaluable assistance made
this book something I am proud of. Andy Boyles inspired
me to be more creative in the writing. My insightful editor,
Alyssa Mito Pusey, helped me refine the book with her
critical eye. Art director Susan Sherman put her heart into
creating a beautiful design that does these creatures
justice. The members of my MC3 critique group provided
thoughtful refinements. Tadpole expert Dr. Ronald Altig
read the manuscript and answered critical questions.
Finally, thanks to my wife, Debbie Carr, who accompanied
me on numerous toading excursions and took the photos
of me with the toads.

Published by Charlesbridge
85 Main Street
Watertown, MA 02472
(617) 926-0329
www.charlesbridge.com

Library of Congress Cataloging-in-Publication Data
Names: Wechsler, Doug, author.
Title: The hidden life of a toad / Doug Wechsler.
Description: Watertown, MA: Charlesbridge, [2017] | Description based
    on print version record and CIP data provided by publisher; resource
    not viewed.
Identifiers: LCCN 2015046143 (print) | LCCN 2015043918 (ebook)
    | ISBN 9781632895752 (ebook) | ISBN 9781632895769 (ebook pdf)
    | ISBN 9781580897389 (reinforced for library use)
Subjects: LCSH: American toad—Life cycles—Juvenile literature.
    | American toad—Behavior—Juvenile literature. | CYAC: Toads.
Classification: LCC QL668.E227 (print) | LCC QL668.E227 W43 2017
    (ebook) | DDC 597.8/7—dc23
LC record available at http://lccn.loc.gov/2015046143

Printed in China
(hc) 10 9 8 7 6 5 4 3 2 1

Type set in Museo Serif, designed by Jos Buivenga, exljbris
Color separations by Colourscan Print Co Pte Ltd, Singapore
Printed by 1010 Printing International Limited
    in Huizhou, Guangdong, China
Production supervision by Brian G. Walker
Designed by Susan Mallory Sherman